BREEDERS' BEST™
A KENNEL CLUB BOOK®

Pembroke Welsh Corgi

By Steven Leyerly

BREEDERS' BEST™
A KENNEL CLUB BOOK®

PEMBROKE WELSH CORGI

ISBN: 1-59378-946-7

Copyright © 2005

Kennel Club Books, LLC
308 Main Street, Allenhurst, NJ 07711 USA
Printed in South Korea

PHOTOS BY:
Paulette Braun,
Bernd Brinkmann, Callea Photo,
Juliette Cunliffe, Isabelle Français,
Carol Ann Johnson, Steven Leyerly,
Bill Shelton and Karen Taylor

DRAWINGS BY:
Yolyanko el Habanero

Contents

History of the Pembroke Welsh Corgi

Are you looking for a "below-the-knee" dog who has a foxy expression and is as smart as whip? If so, the Pembroke Welsh Corgi may be just the dog for you! Like the Scottish Terrier, the Corgi is referred to as a big dog in a small package. An ancient breed, the Corgi hails from the south-western corner of Wales. He is a herding dog, classified in the United States in the Herding Group and in the Pastoral Group in Great

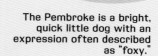

The Pembroke is a bright, quick little dog with an expression often described as "foxy."

Britain. As a herding dog, he was used on Welsh farms to keep the livestock where they belonged, in the proper pastures, and to assist the farmer in taking the animals to market. It is said that every Welsh farm had one or two Corgi-type dogs.

As with most pure-bred dogs, the historical background of the breed is murky and there is little definite information until the more recent past. However, it is known that the Corgi is one of the older dog breeds, unlike many others who can trace their beginnings only back to around the mid-19th century.

There have been legends and theories as to the background of the Corgi. One tale tells of two young children who found two puppies that looked like little foxes. They brought them home and told their parents that the pups were given to them by the fairies and, as the puppies grew, they learned to look after the cattle. The

The Pembroke is a small but sturdy dog, with a body that is low to the ground and moderately long.

The Pembroke is a popular sight at dog shows. Due to his short stature, he is put up on a table for judging to make it easier for the judge to give a full hands-on evaluation.

coloring over the Corgi's shoulders is said to be the saddle used by the fairy riders.

A more realistic theory points to ancient origins, as there are small, short-coated dogs depicted on Egyptian tombs that could be the ancestors of the Corgi. Some feel that the breed was in existence in Wales in 920 AD, when the unwritten Welsh laws were codified and a value was placed upon dogs that worked. The dog referred to as the "herdsman cur" was noted to be of the same value as an ox. Since the Corgi was the only cattle dog in Wales, it was felt that the word "cur" was referring to the Corgi.

Yet another possible origin was put forth in a series of articles that appeared in the *American Kennel Gazette* in 1935, written by W. Lloyd-Thomas, who stated that the Corgi was a member of the family of spitz dogs that were introduced into Wales by the Flemish weavers. Clifford Hubbard, a well-known dog man of England, had his own take on the Corgi's origins in his in-depth study about the Pembroke's beginnings going back to the 9th and 10th centuries, when the Vikings invaded Wales. The Corgi is similar in appearance to the Swedish Vallhund, which Hubbard credits as a near relative of the Pembroke along with the Schipperke and Pomeranian, which was a much larger dog at that time. One other theory put forth by Iris Combe is that the Pembroke bears a close likeness to the Lundehund breed, found on a remote island off Norway.

As complicated as all of these differing theories may be, the Corgi has proven his worth not only as a working dog but also as a pet. The Pembroke Welsh Corgi is here to stay and is a popular pet on both sides of the Atlantic, whether he is herding a flock of sheep, running through the agility course with his owner or sitting on the couch amid his beloved family.

The earliest record for "curs" shown at an agricultural show in England appeared in 1892 in Wales. The name "Corgi" was not seen until an English Kennel Club show in Camarthen, Wales in 1925 had official classes for the breed. In December of the same year, the Corgi Club was formed, with most of the members residing in the Pembrokeshire area of Wales.

It should be noted that there is another Corgi breed, the Cardigan Welsh Corgi, which finds its roots farther north in Wales than the Pembroke. Although there was much inbreeding between the two breeds, they evolved into two separate breeds and descended from different origins. The Cardigan Welsh Corgi, although looking like the Pembroke at first glance, is really quite different. The most noticeable difference to the novice is that the Cardigan has a naturally long tail and the Pembroke has a docked tail.

The first breed standard was written in 1925, the same year that Corgis were offered classes at a Kennel Club show. We've mentioned that, the following year, a group of fanciers formed the Corgi Club. Their first meeting was held at Haverfordwest in southern Wales. That same year, The Kennel Club directed that the club be named the Welsh Corgi Club; the club was then officially registered with The Kennel Club. The breed was recognized by The Kennel Club two years later in 1928, and the

The other Welsh Corgi, the Cardigan, has a long tail that hangs down when the dog is resting. There are other physical distinctions as well, not to mention the dogs' different ancestries.

Pembrokes and Cardigans were shown in the same classes.

In 1928, The Kennel Club moved the Corgi from the "Any Other Variety not Classified" Group into the Non-sporting Group. They were then eligible for Challenge Certificates, awards that make up a British championship, so this meant that the Corgi was truly becoming established. In 1934, The Kennel Club deemed that the two types of Corgis were actually two separate breeds and from that time on, they were shown either as Pembroke Welsh Corgis or Cardigan Welsh Corgis. Until that time, there had been hard feelings between fanciers of the two types; if a judge at a show was a Cardigan breeder, the Pembroke people refused to show their dogs under him.

With the 1934 ruling plus The Kennel Club's allowing tail docking at that time, the Pembroke was on its way to becoming a very popular dog in the UK when the Duke of York, who became King George VI, bought a Pembroke for his daughters, Princesses Elizabeth and Margaret. This caused the breed to become firmly established as a part of the British scene. The Pembroke Welsh Corgi is still the favorite breed of the Queen. She keeps several dogs with her at all times and tends to their needs herself. The journalists' interest in the British royal family and their doings has certainly contributed greatly to the popularity of this breed.

The Pembroke has not just enjoyed popularity in its homeland. In 1930, the Rozavel kennel of Mrs. Thelma Gray appeared on the scene in England. Mrs. Gray promoted the breed on both sides of the Atlantic and founded the Welsh Corgi League in England, which is still a very active club with a large membership. Rozavel dogs were prominent in the pedigrees of many American dogs for many decades.

One of the first Pembrokes to come to the United States was imported by Mrs. Lewis Roesler, whose first encounter with the breed was at Paddington Station in London, when she saw a Corgi who was traveling by train to a dog show. Mrs. Roesler immediately purchased this bitch, Little Madam, and brought her home to the US to add to her Merriedip Kennels of Old English Sheepdogs. Through the years, Mrs. Roesler continued to bring back top Corgis (and Old English) whenever she traveled to England.

When the breed was recognized in America, Mrs. Roesler's bitch, Little Madam of Merriedip, became the first Corgi to be registered in the American Kennel Club (AKC) Stud Book. The first litter to be registered with the AKC was whelped in August 1934 from Canadian-bred dogs and owned by Mr. E. M. Tidd of Oakland, California.

In 1935, Mr. Tidd purchased Bowhit Pivot, a Best-in-Show winner in

Winning handler and Pembroke with the "Welsh Dragon" at a show hosted by the Welsh Kennel Club. What at first glance appears to be a wreath around the dog's neck is actually the tail of a dragon statue.

England, from Lord Hothfield in Wales. This dog became the first Pembroke to achieve a Group win in the United States. Named Ch. Sierra Bowhit Pivot in the US, he was eventually purchased by Derek Rayne, a well-known AKC judge and

Corgi breeder, and then became the first Corgi in the US to add an obedience title to his name. Pivot lived a long life, sired five champions and won a Group at the age of seven.

At first, the Pembroke was classified by the AKC as a terrier and was shown in the Terrier Group. Breeders from several terrier breeds were helpful in promoting the Corgi, especially some Sealyham Terrier breeders in Wales and a group of American Cairn Terrier breeders. Shortly after, the breed was transferred to the Working Group until the Herding and Working dogs were separated. Now both Welsh Corgis are aptly

classified in the AKC's Herding Group.

The parent club for the breed, the Pembroke Welsh Corgi Club of America, was formed in 1936. The club's aim was and still is to protect the best interests of the breed and preserve its true qualities through careful breeding, as well as to educate the public about the Pembroke.

During the years of World War II, the Pembroke suffered, as did many breeds, as dog shows were seldom held and breeding was greatly curtailed for a variety of reasons. However, by the mid-1940s, dogs were again being imported from England, many from the aforementioned Rozavel kennels. The first Pembroke to win an all-breed Best in Show in the US was Rozavel Uncle Sam of Waseeka, who followed his win with second place in the Group at the 1949 Westminster Kennel Club show.

Since the early days of the

The Pembroke continues to rack up impressive wins in the US, in its homeland and around the world.

breed, Pembroke Welsh Corgis have remained popular and dearly beloved dogs of both the British and the Americans. In 1963, the Walt Disney film, *Little Dog Lost,* featuring a Corgi, sparked more interest in the breed from the American public and registrations rose temporarily. However, the breed has been fortunate on both sides of the Atlantic to have retained its popularity without any large surges, as these dramatic rises in popularity can often be very detrimental to a breed. At the present time, the Pembroke Welsh Corgi remains between 20th and 25th in popularity of the AKC breeds, based on registration statistics, and shows little movement toward more or less popularity. The breed is fortunate to have breeders who continue to strive for exceptional stock in conformation, health and disposition.

HISTORY OF THE PEMBROKE WELSH CORGI

Overview

- One of the smaller of the herding breeds, the Pembroke hails from Wales, where he was a staple on the farms and performed various tasks to help the farmers with livestock.
- From the mythical to the factual, many possible origins of the breed have been put forth.
- At first the two Welsh Corgis, the Pembroke and the Cardigan, were shown together but they were eventually separated into distinct breeds by England's Kennel Club.
- Britain's royal family brought the Pembroke into the public eye.
- Several important kennels in the US got started with UK stock. The breed caught on in the US with some important show wins and has retained popularity without becoming overly popular.

Description of the Pembroke

Every breed of dog registered with the American Kennel Club has an official written breed standard. This standard is an official document that details what the breed should look and act like. The Pembroke Welsh Corgi standard has been formulated by the breed's national parent club, the Pembroke Welsh Corgi Club of America (PWCCA), and you can find the complete standard on the AKC's website, www.akc.org.

The Pembroke Welsh Corgi is a big dog in a small package. He may not come up to your knee in height but

Not just a herding dog but also a cuddler extraordinaire, this "big dog in a small package" appeals to many people with its wonderful companion qualities.

he is a tough, strong, active and intelligent dog that is more than capable of putting in a hard day's work before relaxing indoors with the family at night. He should never appear in looks to be "overdone" and, of utmost importance, he is neither shy nor vicious.

This dog possesses the characteristic "intelligent and interested" expression, erect ears and balanced, strong little body.

In size, he is between 10 and 12 inches in height at the shoulder and weighs no more than 30 pounds for males and 28 pounds for bitches. The standard notes that the dog is moderately long and low, but he should appear neither coarse nor racy.

Although his head is foxy in shape and appearance, the Pembroke should not look "sly." His eyes are neither round nor protruding and they are brown in color, in a shade that complements his coat color. Black eye rims are preferred but the black eye itself is not desirable. The ears of a Pembroke are important and they should be upright, not floppy, of

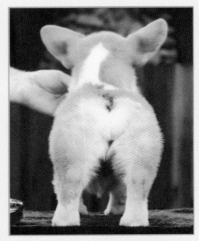

Even a puppy's hindquarters should be "strong and flexible, moderately angulated" and legs should be parallel to each other when viewed from behind.

medium size and rounded at the points. The standard notes that "a line drawn from the nose tip through the eyes to the ear tips, and across, should form an approximate equilateral triangle."

The Pembroke has a fairly long neck that is slightly arched and of the proper length to give balance, as a very short neck will give him a "stuffy" appearance. He has a

This regal Corgi exudes the "bold but kind" temperament mentioned in the standard.

deep chest that comes down between the forelegs. The tail is docked as short as possible but sometimes a pup is born with a natural dock; if short enough, a naturally docked tail is acceptable.

His feet turn neither in nor out and feet that are too round, long and narrow or splayed are considered faulty. Usually the dewclaws (the "fifth toes") are removed from both the front and rear legs. He should be a well-muscled dog; remember, he was originally a herding dog and is expected to be able to trot up and down the pasture all day, taking care of the livestock, whether he actually is used in this capacity or not.

The Pembroke's coat is medium in length, made up of a weather-resistant undercoat with a coarse and longer outer coat that lies flat. Pembrokes shed heavily once or twice a year, and often a bitch will shed her coat after having a litter of puppies. A "marcelled" (wavy) coat is considered a fault, as is a too-short coat or a thin coat.

and a narrow blaze on the head is also acceptable. Mismarks include white on the

Puppies have much developing to do before they will meet the specifications described in the standard, but experienced breeders can evaluate young pups for their future potential as show or breeding dogs.

His colors are red, sable, fawn, black and tan, with or without white markings. White is permitted on the legs, chest, neck, muzzle and underparts, back between the withers and tail, white on the sides between the elbows and back of the hindquarters or white on the ears.

The Pembroke should have a free and smooth gait; his hind legs should show drive and move on a line with the forelegs. In the section on gait, the standard notes, "This is a herding dog, which must have the agility, freedom of movement and endurance to do the work for which he was developed." The standard also states, "Outlook bold, but kindly. Never shy or vicious. The judge shall dismiss from the ring any Pembroke Welsh Corgi that is excessively shy."

The following are considered serious faults in the Pembroke Welsh Corgi: oversized or undersized; button, rose or drop ears; overshot or undershot bite; fluffies (dogs with coats of extreme length with exaggerated feathering); whitelies (dogs with white body color with red or dark

Although the Pembroke's legs may be short, they can cover great distances with endurance and agility.

markings) and bluies (dogs in which the colored portions of the coat have a distinct bluish or smoky cast).

Do note, however, that these serious faults pertain to the show and/or breeding dog. When breeders have puppies with minor esthetic faults, such as less-than-perfect markings or not-quite-right ear shape, they will sell these well-bred pups into pet homes. Such "pet-quality" pups may fall short in certain beauty points, but are still as healthy and sound as their show-potential litter-mates. Most breeders require owners of pet-quality pups to sign a spay/neuter contract, agreeing to have the dogs altered at the appropriate age, as only top-quality members of the breed that adhere very closely to the standard should be bred.

DESCRIPTION OF THE PEMBROKE

Overview

- The Pembroke can be summed up as a "big dog in a small package." His body is somewhat long and low to the ground, but it should be balanced and not exaggerated in any way.
- The Pembroke is known for his "foxy" appearance, complemented by brown eyes, erect ears and dark pigmentation.
- The breed's feet and legs are designed for endurance; this is a well-muscled dog whose fore- and hindquarters are balanced.
- The Pembroke's medium-length double coat is seen in a variety of colors, but certain colors/markings and too-long coats are serious faults for show dogs.
- Temperament is also mentioned in the standard; this is as important as the physical characteristics and is described as "bold but kindly."

Are You a Pembroke Person?

The Pembroke Welsh Corgi is not just a herding dog—he is also a companion dog and he can be one of the best! In addition to his herding skills, he has been bred to be a loving and well-behaved companion with an even disposition. In the Herding Group, he finds himself with the other canines that have been bred to herd and tend sheep, goats and cattle. Of course, the Pembroke's size sets him apart from the other breeds in the group, as he is the smallest of

Are you ready to open your heart and home to this handsome herder from Wales, a spirited dog with a personality much bigger than he is?

all herding dogs. His primary job as a working dog is to nip at the heels of the cattle to keep them in line: to keep them in their pasture, return them to the barn or help the farmer take them to market. Thus his small size came in handy as he could nip at the cattle's heels and then dodge out of the way of kicking hooves.

Before purchasing your Corgi, you must give some thought to the personality and characteristics of this dog to determine whether this is the breed for you. Even if not used for herding, the Pembroke will retain his breed's instincts. You must consider how these instincts will translate into a pet home. As you are researching the Pembroke breed, here are some of the questions you should ask yourself as you are considering your decision:

1. Do you have the time to give to a dog? Your Pembroke will need care, companionship, training and grooming. Owning a dog is like

Do you wish to show your Pembroke or participate in other activities with him? This is a breed with potential to succeed in many areas of canine competition.

Small enough to "baby," yet sturdy and athletic, the Pembroke appeals to many types of owners.

having a child, except that the dog remains childlike in that he will always be totally dependent on you for his care.

2. Do you have a fenced-in yard for your Corgi? This is not a breed that you can leave tied out on the porch. Even though he is a small dog, he must have a secure area in which to run and exercise.

3. Will you be willing to work with your dog in basic obedience training? Are you prepared to see that he becomes a proper canine citizen with good manners?

4. Are you looking for a pet that will be a companion, that will live in the house with you and that will want to spend his waking hours with the family?

5. Have you owned a dog previously and did that dog live a long and happy life with you?

6. Do you have children at home and are you willing to teach and supervise them so

that they will not mistreat their pet?

7. Will your neighbors be upset by a vocal dog? If your Pembroke's barking becomes excessive, are you willing to train your dog so that he will not be a nuisance?

8. Although this is a breed that will require little grooming, will you take the time to care for his basic grooming and hygiene needs?

Let's now look at the answers to these questions, one at a time:

1. Time for a dog does not mean that you cannot work and own a dog. Your Corgi will need attention and quality time with you, just as a child needs it. He must be fed on a regular schedule and exercised several times a day. He needs to be petted and loved, and he will like to accompany you to different places whenever possible. You must work with him to have an obedient dog with good manners. Your Pembroke

Once you've decided that the Pembroke is indeed the breed for you, and you are the right person for the breed, you can begin your search for a puppy from a reputable breeder.

should have a minimum of two good outings a day, meaning at least a walk or romp in the morning and again in the evening. You also must ensure your dog's safety: never let him out loose to run the neighborhood. Exercise and training must be on-leash or in a safely enclosed area.

2. Speaking of safe enclosures, a fenced yard is ideal for letting your Pembroke run off some energy. A yard should be big enough for you to throw a ball and for your dog to run with it. And remember, it is your responsibility to keep the yard clean of feces. On that note, it is essential to carry a plastic bag or two with you when out walking your dog so that you can pick up droppings. This is not just proper etiquette; in most towns, it's the law.

3. The Pembroke can be a very strong-willed dog, and it will be essential for you to determine as soon as you

bring him home that you, not your dog, are master of the household. If you do not let your Corgi know this, he will very quickly take over the leadership role and start running your household on his terms. Establish early on that everything will be done your way.

4. Hopefully you are interested in a dog because you want to spend time with your dog. The Pembroke is a dog that likes companionship and likes to be with his family. You cannot just leave a Pembroke out in the yard for hours and expect him to be content. He likely will find ways to entertain himself, though, but his ideas of amusement are likely not what you will consider acceptable behavior (barking, digging, etc.).

5. Previous experience with dog ownership will give you a good idea of what a dog expects from you and what you must do for your dog. If

this is your first time owning a Corgi, you must know that this is an active dog with definite herding instincts, even if kept solely as a pet. He who will put up with a certain amount of tail-tugging and ear-pulling from a youngster—not so with a Corgi! You will have to teach

Pembrokes love their people and aren't afraid to show it! Although this is a working herding breed by nature, don't discount your Pembroke's need to be a true member of the family.

will need exercise and lessons in manners. This is a smart dog and needs an owner who is equally as smart as, or smarter than, he is!

6. The Pembroke will not tolerate, nor should he be expected to, any mistreatment from a child, unlike a Labrador or Golden Retriever, your children how to behave toward and around this pet. This includes no running around wildly, lest they incite his herding instincts and he attempts to round up his "flock," which can mean a child's ankles getting nipped in the process. This is not aggressive behavior on the

Corgi's part, just instinctive behavior that must be considered and controlled. So, you can see that both Corgi and child need to be supervised and taught how to interact properly with each other.

7. The Pembroke can be a bit noisy if he is given the chance. Corgis can have a tendency to bark, just to hear the sound of their own voices! Therefore, you must train your Corgi not to bark needlessly, as this will not foster good relationships with your neighbors.

8. Although grooming is minimal with this breed, your Pembroke will need to have his coat brushed out on a regular basis, probably a few times weekly. Additionally, nails must be clipped, ears and eyes kept clean and teeth brushed as part of his home hygiene routine. You will want to make sure that he is kept clean and smelling nice. Are you willing to take the time to do this with your pet?

In addition to being prized by farmers for his herding abilities, the Corgi is dearly loved by pet owners for his disposition, his intelligence, his convenient size, his good looks and his devotion to his family. This is an alert, lively and very personable breed. While all of these traits sound

Adding a Pembroke to your life means the start of a long and rewarding relationship with one of dogdom's most versatile and personable canine companions.

appealing, the Pembroke is not the right dog for everyone, nor is every household suitable for a Pembroke. Do learn all you can about the breed before rushing out and buying the first puppy you see.

Soak up all the information you can about the Pembroke Welsh Corgi. Read this book from cover to cover and also check out other books on the breed.

Talk to Pembroke owners and meet people in the breed. Although you cannot trust all that you read online, there are excellent and reputable sources of information on the Internet such as the Pembroke Welsh Corgi Club of America's website, www.pembrokecorgi.org, or the American Kennel Club's website, www.akc.org.

ARE YOU A PEMBROKE PERSON?

Overview

- A herding dog by trade, the Pembroke is best known these days as a wonderful pet and home companion.
- Owners of a Pembroke must take into consideration his intelligence as well as his herding instincts, which will still be part of his character whether he is used for work or not.
- You must have the time to care for your Pembroke, give him lots of attention and provide for his safety. These are essential for ownership of any dog.
- If you have kids, teaching the dog and children to respect each other is important. Otherwise, the kids may play too roughly with the dog or your Corgi may try to "herd" the kids.
- Learn all about the breed, good and bad, to make an honest assessment about your suitability for the Pembroke and vice versa.

Selecting a Breeder

You want the Pembroke that you choose to grow up into a happy, well-adjusted member of the breed and of your family.

When you start your search for a Pembroke puppy, you will be looking for a healthy puppy from a responsible breeder. A responsible breeder is someone who is experienced in the breed and puts considerable thought into each and every mating. The responsible breeder does extensive research before breeding his dog or bitch. He considers health problems in the breed, has room in his home or kennel for a litter of puppies and has the time to dedicate to a litter. He does not breed to the dog down the block because it is easy and the two dogs are cute; he does not have a litter to show his children all about the miracle of birth. A responsible breeder is someone who is dedicated to the Pembroke breed and to eliminating faults and hereditary problems through health screening and very selective breeding. This type of breeder knows all about the potential genetic problems in the breed, has appropriate testing done and only breeds healthy animals. The Corgi can be prone to eye problems, including progressive retinal atrophy, juvenile cataracts and persistent pupillary membrane. The breeder should show you clearances from the Canine Eye Registration Foundation, showing that the parents of the litter have been tested as free of these problems. Likewise, the parents should have Orthopedic Foundation for Animals certification, proving

Even a youngster will possess the curious and intelligent expression typical of the Pembroke.

A good breeder will be someone who truly loves the Pembroke breed and gives the best of care to her dogs.

no hip dysplasia. Other concerns in the Pembroke include von Willebrand's disease, a blood-clotting disorder, and degenerative myelopathy, a spinal cord disorder that is currently the subject of intensive research. Visit the PWCCA's website for

Quality shines in a well-bred Corgi, as exhibited in this four-and-a-half-month-old puppy from Coventry kennels.

more on what you should look for when purchasing a puppy.

A responsible breeder's priority is to improve the breed by producing healthy, sound, top-quality puppies. He will study pedigrees and see what the leading stud

dogs are producing. To find the right stud dog for his bitch, he may fly his bitch across the country to breed to a particular stud dog, or he may drive the bitch to a good stud dog who may be located a considerable distance away. This breeder may only have one or two litters a year, which means that there may not be a puppy ready for you when you first call. Remember that you are purchasing a new family member and usually the wait will be well worth it!

Check out the PWCCA's website for a listing of regional Pembroke Corgi clubs; there are 15 or so across the country. If there is a club in your part of the country, it should be able to help you find a responsible member breeder in your region. You can also access a list of PWCCA member breeders directly from the club's website. The responsible Pembroke Welsh Corgi breeder will probably be someone who has been breeding for some years and someone who is known on the national level. He will be a member of his local Pembroke Welsh Corgi club, providing that there is one, and will also belong to the PWCCA. Member breeders are obliged to uphold the club's code of ethics in their breeding program. By acquainting yourself with the national and regional clubs, and by contacting breeders in your area, you will be able to do your breeder research and also get answers to any questions about the breed that you may have.

When it comes time to visit some breeders, the responsible breeder will show you his kennel, if he has a kennel, or will invite you into his home to see the puppies. The areas will be clean and smell good. The breeder will show you the dam of the litter that you are looking at and she will be clean and healthy. The puppies will also be clean, with tidy toenails and clean faces. The breeder may

Good breeders will be able to evaluate a pup's show potential by predicting how well he will mature into a good-quality Pembroke that will adhere closely to the breed standard.

not show you the entire litter, as he may not want to show you the puppies that have already been sold or that he is going to keep for himself for potential showing or future breeding.

You will be checking out the breeder, but the responsible breeder will also have many questions for you. He will have an adoption application for you to fill out and will interview you at length. Have you had a dog before? How many have you owned and have you ever owned a Corgi? Why are you interested in having a Corgi as a pet? Did your dogs live long lives? Do you have a fenced yard? How many children do you have and what are their ages? Are you willing to spend time to teach your children how to

One look at a young Corgi's sweet face and you will be hooked! However, you have to use your head, not just your heart, in choosing a breeder and puppy.

treat the new family member? Have you ever done any dog training and are you willing to go to obedience classes with your Corgi? Are there any other pets in your household? Where will the dog sleep and where will he spend time when home alone? Do you currently have a vet and can he provide references?

Do not be offended by these questions. The breeder has put a lot of research, time, effort and money into this and every litter, and his first priority is to place each pup

in caring and suitable households where the pups will be wanted, loved and cared for properly.

Temperament tests include observing how the pup reacts to certain types of handling.

SELECTING A BREEDER

Overview

- Learn what makes a responsible breeder and realize that this is your only source from which to consider a Pembroke puppy.
- Good breeders are dedicated to improving the breed by carefully selecting their breeding stock based on soundness, temperament, health and conformation.
- The national breed club as well as the regional Pembroke clubs are trusted sources for breeder referrals, but you must still meet these breeders and check them out yourself.
- A good breeder will be assessing you as a prospective owner just as carefully as you are assessing him as a breeder.

CHAPTER 5

Finding the Right Puppy

A barrel of gorgeous puppies from Coventry kennels: selection doesn't get any better or harder than this!

Before meeting the breeder and seeing his pups, you should have given some consideration as to whether you want a male or a female Pembroke for a pet. Some individuals consider males to be easier to train but the more dominant of the two sexes. Others prefer the softer disposition of the female. In the Pembroke Corgi, the male will be a few pounds heavier and an inch or two taller than the female, but neither sex is a large dog.

If you do not plan to neuter or spay your pet (although you should, and some breeders will require you to neuter or spay a pet-only Pembroke at the appropriate age), females will come into season approximately every six months. This can be a difficult time for up to three weeks as it is fairly messy, is hard on the house and will attract any roaming Romeos in the neighborhood, who will sit on your doorstep like lovelorn swains. Males who are not neutered can be more determined and will have more of a tendency to lift their legs and to try to mount your leg. Of course, with the stature of a Corgi, he will probably get to your ankle rather than your leg! If you are not sure which sex you prefer, or if you really have no preference, discuss it with the breeder and he will be able to give you some direction.

If you are a first-time puppy owner, do know that there will be

The belly-up posture is a submissive one. Once a pup is comfortable, though, he may roll onto his back to ask for a belly rub, a favorite of many dogs.

Pembroke puppies are undeniably cuddly and huggable!

CHAPTER 5

expenses in addition to the price of the puppy. You will need collars, leashes, dog dishes and grooming tools. A dog crate is really essential as well as sturdy fencing of sufficient height and embedded into the ground to make the yard truly escape-proof. For a small breed like the Corgi, the expenses can be less than those incurred with a large breed, as larger crates and higher fencing are more expensive.

With all of these things in mind, you are now ready to select your puppy. You have decided that you are a Pembroke Welsh Corgi person and that you can live with this very alert, courageous, smart and active dog. Your entire family is ready for this new arrival to come into your home, lives and hearts. You have done your homework and have located a responsible breeder who has a litter available. When that exciting time comes to meet with the breeder, you arrive at the appointed time and the breeder has the puppies ready for you to see. They should be a happy bunch. Their noses will be wet, their coats will have a glow and they will have a nice covering of flesh over their ribs. You will be ready to pick up one of these adorable rascals and cuddle him in your arms.

Before you let your heart get the best of you, get to know the pups. When looking over the pups that you are shown, take time to observe their behavior and their interactions with each other, the breeder and you. Do not pick the puppy that hangs back and think twice before picking the extra-active, most outgoing of the litter. However, do keep in mind that in this breed, all puppies will be quite active, and some of them even a bit hyper! While all pups should be energetic and full of life, overly hyper puppies can turn into hyper adults who will require more patience and time in training. Look for the middle-of-the-road puppy, the one that is interested, comes up to you, listens when you speak and looks very alert.

you want one that is bright, healthy, even-tempered and personable.

You should ask the breeder whether the sire and dam of the litter have had their temperaments tested.

When you approach the litter, first observe them from a distance and watch how they interact with each other.

Never, but never pick the pup that shies away and will not approach you. Never pick a puppy because you "feel sorry" for him. Don't forget that you are adding a new member to your family and

These tests are offered by the American Temperament Test Society (ATTS). Responsible breeders will be familiar with this organization and will have had their animals tested. The breeder will show you the score sheet and you can easily determine if the parents of the litter are dogs with the types of personalities you are seeking. In addition, temperament testing is an excellent indication that this is a responsible breeder.

Temperament testing by the ATTS is done on dogs that are at least 18 months of age; therefore, puppies are not tested but the sire and dam of a litter can be tested. The test is like a simulated walk through a park or a neighborhood where everyday situations are encountered. Neutral, friendly and threatening situations are presented to observe and assess the dog's reactions to the various stimuli. Problems that are looked for are unprovoked aggression, panic without recovery and strong avoidance. Behavior toward strangers, reaction to auditory, visual and tactile stimuli and self-protective and aggressive behavior are observed. The dog is on a loose lead for the test, which takes about ten minutes to complete. Recent ATTS statistics shows 171 Pembrokes tested in a given year, with 133 having passed the test, for a 78% passing rate. This is consistent scoring compared to years prior.

Some breeders will have the temperaments of their puppies tested by either a professional, their veterinarian or another dog breeder. They will find the high-energy pup and the pup that is slower to respond. They will find the pup with the independent spirit and the one that will want to follow the pack. Even if the litter has not been tested, the breeder will know the pups well and will be able to make an educated suggestion as to which pup he thinks will be best for your family.

If the litter has not been tested, you can do a few simple tests while you are sitting on the floor playing with the pups. Pat your leg or snap your finger and see which pup comes up to you first. Clap your hands and see if one of the litter shies away from you. See how they play with one another. Watch for the one that has the personality that you find most appealing, as this will probably be the puppy that you will take home. Look for the puppy that appears to be "in the middle," not rambunctious, aggressive or overly submissive.

If you know that you want a Pembroke, but are not sure that you want to raise a puppy, you do have other options. One of these is to adopt an adult "rescue" Corgi. This will be a dog who, for a wide variety of reasons, is looking for a new home. This will usually be a dog over one year of age and very often trained and housebroken, at least to some extent. The breed rescue organization

consists of a network of foster homes in which the dogs are cared for, socialized and given veterinary attention while awaiting new permanent homes. Usually these dogs make marvelous pets, as they are grateful for another chance to live in loving

Whether you adopt a puppy from a breeder or rescue an adult, Corgi ownership will be a rewarding experience for you and your family.

homes. Not only does the national club have an active rescue organization but the local clubs also have groups of caring individuals working in this capacity. Rescue committees consist of very dedicated individuals who care deeply about the breed and give countless hours of their time and money to assure that each dog will have an equal chance at a good life with a family who loves him. As with a breeder, you will have to fill out an application and be approved by the rescue to adopt one of their dogs. Likewise, you will want to investigate the background of a rescue dog as much as possible so that you understand his living situation and behavior up to this point. By going through the Pembroke Welsh Corgi Club of America's rescue organization, you should be assured of getting a dog that you will be able to live with happily. Links to Pembroke rescue organizations can be found on the PWCCA's website as well as on the websites of the individual Pembroke clubs.

One other option is that the breeder may have an older dog that he wants to place in a good home. For some breeders, once they have put a championship on a dog, they would like to move this animal into a

Every Corgi deserves a loving, permanent home. Plenty of outdoor activity will keep the Pembroke's body fit, mind alert and instincts keen.

home where the dog will receive the optimum of attention. Do give this some thought, as often a retired show dog will be very well trained and easy to live with.

Whether you are leaning toward a puppy or an adult, take some time with your choice. If you are at all hesitant, tell the breeder that you would like to go home and think it over. This is a major decision, as you are adding a family member who should be with you for at least 10 years, likely closer to 15. Be sure that you get the Pembroke that everyone in your household will be happy with. Once you decide, you will be ready to embark on a rewarding and fulfilling relationship with a dog of a wonderful breed.

FINDING THE RIGHT PUPPY

Overview

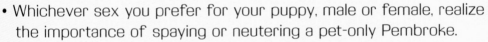
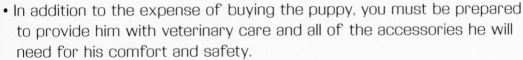

- Whichever sex you prefer for your puppy, male or female, realize the importance of spaying or neutering a pet-only Pembroke.
- In addition to the expense of buying the puppy, you must be prepared to provide him with veterinary care and all of the accessories he will need for his comfort and safety.
- Use your head, not just your heart, when selecting your puppy. Observe the pups, get to know their personalities and make sure they all are healthy; ask the breeder to show you health-testing documentation.
- The breeder may have done formal temperament testing or may evaluate the pups using his own expertise. Either way, he will be able to guide you toward a pup that suits you.
- To add an adult Pembroke to your life, contact a breed club's rescue organization or ask breeders about retired show dogs who may be seeking pet homes.

Welcoming the Pembroke Puppy

Your Pembroke will welcome an array of safe chew toys as a puppy and as an adult.

You are now about to bring your puppy home and welcome him as a new family member. If you are driving some distance to pick up your pet, take along a towel or two, a water bowl, some water and your pup's leash and collar with his new ID tags attached. Also take along some plastic baggies and a roll of paper towels in case you make any bathroom pit stops, or in case the pup has a potty accident in the car or experiences carsickness. You want to be prepared to clean up! No matter how far you are traveling, you should either arrange for someone to accompany you so that he can hold the puppy on the way home or have a travel crate with you to keep the puppy safe and secure.

A wire crate provides good ventilation, a view of his surroundings and a feeling of security for the new puppy.

PREPARING FOR YOUR PUP

Before your puppy comes home, you have many preparations to make. You should have all of the necessary accessories on hand, such as food and water bowls, a leash, a collar and a crate for use in the home. Your puppy will be trained not only to sleep in his crate but also to feel comfortable spending time there when he is home alone or unsupervised. In very short order, he will learn that the crate is his second "home," and he will feel safe and at ease when he is in his own private "house." If the pup is left alone and uncrated, he will be able to do a lot

Along with your new puppy comes all of the things that the puppy needs! These items include a leash, a collar, grooming equipment, bowls, toys and more.

of damage. Puppies often like to chew on furniture, corners of woodwork, shoes left out, etc. Keeping him in a confined area when you cannot supervise will eliminate these problems and, most importantly, keep your puppy out of danger. Be sure to add several towels or a washable blanket to the crate so that he will be comfortable. Here's a more detailed look at your puppy-accessory needs:

Food and water bowls: You'll need two separate serving pieces, one for food and one for water. Stainless steel pans are your best choice as they are chew-proof and easy to clean. Tip-proof is a good idea too, since most puppies love to splash about in their water bowls, and the Pembroke is no exception.

Puppy food: Your Pembroke puppy should be fed a quality food that is appropriate for his age and breed. Most premium dog foods now offer breed-specific formulas that address the nutritional needs of different-sized breeds of dog during the various stages of their lives. Your Corgi puppy will start with a puppy growth food, which should be his diet for his first year. While the protein and fat content of a growth-formula food will be higher than that of an adult-maintenance food, the food should not encourage rapid growth. A good puppy food promotes healthy growth at a steady pace.

Your Pembroke's early growth period as well as his long-term health will benefit from a diet of high-quality puppy and dog food. Canine nutrition is addressed in greater detail in a later chapter on proper feeding. For recommendations, check with your breeder and your vet before you buy your puppy's food. Your breeder will likely even send you home with some of the food that the pup has been eating.

Collar and ID tag: Your Pembroke pup should have an adjustable collar that expands to fit him as he grows. Lightweight yet durable nylon adjustable collars work best for both pups and adult dogs. Put the collar on as soon as your pup comes home so he can get used to wearing it. The ID tag, which must be attached to his everyday collar at all times, should have your phone number, name and address, but not the puppy's name, as that would enable a stranger to identify and call your dog. Some owners include a line that says "Dog needs medication" to hopefully speed the dog's return if he is lost or stolen. Attach the tag with an "O" ring (the kind used in key rings), as the more common "S" ring snags on carpets and comes off easily.

Today, even dog collars have gone high-tech. Some come equipped with beepers and tracking devices. The most advanced pet identification tool uses a Global Positioning System and fits inside a collar or tag. When your dog leaves his programmed home perimeter, the device sends a message directly to your phone or email address.

Choke collars or other

It may take some time to convince a mouthy pup that his leash is for wearing, not chewing.

training collars are not necessary for young pups and should certainly never be left on a dog, as this is dangerous. A nylon everyday collar will suffice for teaching him how to walk on lead as a youngster. Later, if you feel that a training collar is needed, ask for advice from your breeder or a trainer to help you choose and use one properly.

Leashes: For your puppy's safety and your own convenience, you should have two kinds of leads for him. A narrow six-foot leather or woven nylon leash is best for house-training, walks, puppy training classes and learning to walk properly on leash. The other is a retractable lead. This is an extendable lead that is housed in a large plastic handle; it extends or retracts with the push of a button. Retractable leads are available in several lengths (8 feet to 26 feet) and for different weight ranges, so be sure to buy one that will suit your Pembroke's adult weight. Longer is better, as it allows your dog to run about and check out the good sniffing areas farther away from you. These leads are especially handy for exercising your puppy in unfenced areas or when traveling with your dog.

Crating and gating: These will be your most important puppy purchases. A crate is the most valuable tool for house-breaking your pup, and your pup's favorite place to feel secure. Crates come in three varieties: wire, fabric mesh and the familiar plastic or fiberglass airline-type design. Wire or fabric-mesh crates offer the best ventilation and some conveniently fold up suitcase-style. A fabric-mesh crate might, however, be a little risky for the youngster who likes to dig and chew.

Whatever your choice, purchase an adult-sized crate, as your Pembroke will soon grow into it and will quickly outgrow a puppy-sized crate. Length is the most important measurement when choosing a crate for a full-grown Pembroke; usually a 32-inch long crate will be a good fit. Crates often come with removable divider panels so you can create a smaller area for the pup and expand it as he grows. A too-large crate will not be useful for house-training nor will it be a cozy den if the pup feels lost in it! Crates are available at most pet stores and through pet-supply catalogs.

Well-placed baby gates will protect your house from the inevitable puppy mischief and thus save your sanity as well. It's wise to confine the puppy to a tiled or uncarpeted room or space, ideally one that is accessible to the outside door that he will use for potty trips. Gated to a safe area where he has access to his potty exit and cannot wreak havoc or destruction, the puppy will soon master house-training, chew only appropriate chew toys rather than the legs of your antique chair and spare himself unnecessary corrections for the puppy mishaps that would happen if he were allowed to roam freely.

Gated, however, does not mean unsupervised. Pembrokes are bright and curious creatures that bore easily and have been known to entertain themselves by doing a little woodwork (i.e., chewing

on things like doors and cabinetry). If your puppy must be unattended, use his crate. Proper use of the crate for safety and house-training is discussed in detail in the chapter on house-training.

Bedding: Dog beds are just plain fun. Beds run the gamut from small and inexpensive to elegant high-end beds suitable for the most royal of dog breeds. But don't go crazy just yet. Better to save that fancy bed for when your Pembroke is older and less apt to shred it up or make a puddle on it. For puppy bedding, it's best to use a few large towels, a mat or a

You will be at an advantage if your breeder introduced the pups to crates, albeit to a limited extent. Once in your home, however, it's only one pup (or dog) per crate.

blanket that can be laundered easily and often.

Grooming tools: Pembrokes are rather easy-to-groom dogs, and you will need only minimal equipment. For the puppy, a fine-toothed comb and a soft-bristled brush will suffice to gently go over his coat. As he gets older, a bristle brush with stiffer bristles can be used. You want any grooming of the puppy to be very gentle so that he grows to like the process, not run and hide when he sees you with a brush! You will also need tooth-brushing products made for dogs, a canine nail clipper, cotton balls to clean the ears and around the eyes, a gentle shampoo formulated for dogs and absorbent towels. For an adult, you may opt to use a hair dryer made for dogs or your own on the lowest setting following his baths.

Introduce your puppy to gentle grooming early on so he learns to like it. Grooming also helps condition the pup to hands-on attention, which will be invaluable when you have to clean his teeth and ears and clip his nails.

Toys: Puppies love all sorts of fuzzy toys that they can carry about. Many pups will snuggle with their woolly toys as they would with their litter-mates. Eventually, though, most puppies shred their fuzzy stuffed toys, which is your cue to remove them and no longer buy them.

Safe chew objects are a must if you hope to direct your Pembroke's chewing onto acceptable objects and away from your shoes and furniture. Sturdy nylon and rubber toys and hard sterilized bones are excellent "chewcifiers" and come in age-appropriate sizes. All dogs love rawhides, but they can be dangerous if pieces are swallowed and thus should be offered only under supervision. Empty gallon milk jugs and sturdy soft-drink bottles are all-time favorites and, best of all, they're free. However, they usually only last a few minutes before they are punctured by puppy teeth, so discard them as soon as they become damaged.

Shoes, socks and slippers are off-limits since even a smart pup can't distinguish between your old loafers that you allow him to chew and your new Italian leather boots that are strictly forbidden. Also avoid soft, squishy rubber toys or ones with button eyes that could be swallowed in the blink of an eye. Here's another important puppy-toy rule: offer only two or three toys at a time. If you give your puppy a smorgasbord of toys, he will soon become bored with all of them and look for more.

SAFETY AND SETTLING IN

Even more important than buying the necessities for your pup is making sure that your home is a safe place. You must be aware that a small puppy can be like a toddler in terms of getting into mischief and things he shouldn't, and that there are

Puppy Safety at Home

After puppy shopping, you must puppy-proof your house. Pembroke Welsh Corgi pups are naturally curious critters that will investigate everything new, then seek-and-destroy just because it's fun. The message here is—never let your puppy roam your house unsupervised. Scout your house for the following hazards:

Trash Cans and Diaper Pails
These are natural puppy magnets (they know where the good smelly stuff is!).

Medication Bottles, Cleaning Materials, Roach and Rodent Poisons, etc.
Lock these up. You'll be amazed at what a determined puppy can find.

Electrical Cords
Unplug them whenever you can and make the others inaccessible. Injuries from chewed electrical cords are extremely common in young dogs.

Dental Floss, Yarn, Needles and Thread and Other Stringy Stuff
Puppies snuffling about at ground level will find and ingest the tiniest of objects and will end up in surgery. Most vets can tell you stories about the stuff they've surgically removed from puppies' guts.

Toilet Bowl Cleaners
If you have them, throw them out now. All dogs are born with "toilet sonar" and quickly discover that the water there is always cold.

Garage
Beware of antifreeze! It is extremely toxic and even a few drops will kill an adult Pembroke Welsh Corgi, less for a pup. Lock it and all other chemicals well out of reach. Fertilizers can also be toxic to dogs.

Socks and Underwear, Shoes and Slippers, Too
Keep them off the floor and close your closet doors. Puppies love all of these things because they smell like you times ten!

dangers in the household that should be eliminated. Before your puppy comes home, puppy-proof the house!

Electrical wires should be raised off the floor and hidden from view as they are very tempting as chewable objects. Swimming pools can be very dangerous, so make certain that your puppy can't get into, or fall into, the pool. Some barricades will be necessary to prevent an accident. Not all dogs can swim and those with short legs like your Corgi cannot climb out of the pool. Watch your deck railings and make sure that your puppy cannot slip through the openings and fall. Do not have any containers of insecticides, antifreeze, paint remover or any other cleaners or chemicals in places where your puppy can get to them, as these can often have a sweet and desirable taste to a puppy and can bring about fatal results.

If you have young children in the house, they must under-stand that the small puppy is a living being and must be treated gently. They cannot pull his ears, pick him up and drop him or otherwise treat him carelessly. This is your responsibility! A child taught about animals at an early age can become a lifelong compassionate animal lover and owner.

Use your common sense in all of these things. Consider where a young child can get into trouble, and your puppy will be right behind him!

When your puppy comes into the house for the first time (after he has relieved himself outside), let him take a look at his new home and surroundings, and then give him a light meal and some water. When he is tired, bring him outside again and then tuck him into his crate either to take a nap or, hopefully, to sleep through the night.

The first day or two for your puppy should be fairly quiet. He will then have time to get used to his new home, surroundings and family members. The first night, he may cry a bit, but if you put a teddy bear or a soft woolly sweater in his crate, this will give him some warmth and security. A nearby ticking clock or a radio playing soft music can also be helpful. Remember, he has been uprooted from a sibling or two, his mother and his familiar breeder, and he will need a day or two to get used to his new family. If he should cry during the first night, let him be and he will eventually quiet down and sleep. By the third night, he should be well settled in. Have patience and within a week or less, it will seem to you, your family and your puppy that you have all been together for years, and you will be off to an excellent start with your puppy.

WELCOMING THE PEMBROKE PUPPY

Overview

- Prepare for your puppy's arrival by purchasing the items you will need for him and making your home a safe, puppy-proof place.
- The basic accessories you will need include bowls, puppy food, a collar, an ID tag, leashes, a crate and possibly baby gates, grooming tools and toys.
- Puppy-proofing means securing or removing all dangerous items such as electrical cords, fertilizers, household chemicals, sharp objects and the like, having escape-proof fencing around the yard and creating a safe area indoors that the pup can call his own.
- Keep things low-key during pup's first few days at home. On the first day, introduce him to his crate and have him sleep in it overnight.

House-training and Other Basics

Socialization as a puppy is essential if you want your Pembroke to get along with other dogs. This Corgi shares his home with another short-legged friend, a Dachshund.

Socializing your puppy is very important if you want a dog that fits into your home and a dog that is a good companion who is enjoyed by everyone. Socializing a puppy means getting him accustomed to his new home and then to the world around him with all of its different people, places, animals, noises and smells. Take it easy when puppy first comes home. Hold and pet your puppy so that he knows that he is wanted and loved. Do not play with him constantly, though, as he is very young and needs time to rest and sleep. Once he's received the necessary vaccinations, you can begin to introduce him to people outside the family and bring him to new places. In a way, socialization is a type of puppy-proofing, but it actually puppy-proofs your puppy, not your house. Puppy socialization is your Pembroke's insurance policy to a happy, stable adulthood, and is, without question, the most important element in a Pembroke puppy's introduction to the human world.

Children and a Pembroke can be the best of friends if the children are taught how to behave around the dog and vice versa.

SOCIALIZATION AND PUPPY CLASS

A canine's primary socialization period occurs during the puppy's first 20 weeks of life. Frequent interaction with new people, including children, and other dogs is essential at this age. As long as he's complete on his vaccinations, you can start to visit new places (dog-friendly, of course) like parks or even the local grocery-store parking lot where there are many different people. Set a goal of two

While crate-training is the most effective way to house-train, some owners use paper-training to get their puppies started and then progress to outdoor training.

new places a week for the next two months. Keep these new situations non-threatening, upbeat and positive, which will create a positive attitude toward future encounters.

Your puppy will need supervised exposure to children. Puppies of all breeds tend to view little people, like toddlers and small children, as littermates and will attempt to exert the upper paw (a dominance ploy) over them. Even though small, Pembroke pups are energetic. Adult family members should supervise and teach the puppy not to nip at or jump up on the kids, and especially not to "herd" them. If the pup is allowed to treat the kids as his "flock," this behavior will be much harder to control when he reaches adulthood.

Pembrokes are generally good with children; nonetheless, both dog and child must be taught how to play properly with each other, and children must learn to respect their puppy's privacy. Teach the children not to run or otherwise entice the puppy into rambunctious behavior that could lead to unnecessary corrections for the pup.

Take your Pembroke youngster to puppy school. Some classes accept pups as young as 10 to 12 weeks of age, with one series of puppy shots as a health requirement. The younger the pup, the easier it is to shape good behavior patterns. A good puppy class teaches proper canine social etiquette rather than rigid obedience skills. Your puppy will meet and play with young dogs of other breeds, and you will learn about the positive teaching tools you'll need to train your pup. Puppy class is important for both novice and experienced puppy folks. If you're a smart Pembroke owner, you won't stop there and will continue on with a basic obedience class. Of course, you want the best-behaved Pembroke in the neighborhood.

HOUSE-TRAINING

Most puppy owners dread the prospect of house-training their new puppies. Thoughts of piles and puddles on the carpet strike fear into their hearts. But there is an easier way…it's called using the dog crate. Experienced dog owners and trainers emphasize that crates are the most logical and humane approach to house-training. Because canines are natural den creatures, thanks to the thousands of years that their ancestors spent living in caves and cavities in the ground, the crate appeals to their ancestral instincts. In short order, your puppy will consider his crate his personal home-within-a-home and adapt quite naturally to crate confinement. Your Pembroke puppy also is inherently clean and will prefer not to soil his "den" or living space, so the crate is a logical house-training aid.

It's up to you to make sure that the pup's introduction to the crate is a pleasant one. Introduce the crate as soon as he comes home so he learns that this is his new "house." This is best accomplished with dog treats. For the first day or two, toss a tiny treat into the crate to entice him to go in. Pick a crate command, such as

Your Corgi is a bright little dog who should learn the proper potty routine rather quickly if you are consistent in your training.

"Kennel," "Inside" or "Crate," and use it every time he enters. You also can feed his first few meals inside the crate with the door still open, so the crate association will be a happy one.

Your puppy should sleep in his crate from his very first night. He may whine at first and object to the confinement, but be strong and stay the

CHAPTER 7

course. If you release him when he cries, you provide his first life lesson…if I cry, I get out and maybe hugged. Your attention is a reward for his crying, so you'll see why that's not such a good plan after all.

A better scheme is to place the crate next to your bed at night for the first few weeks. Your presence will comfort him, and you'll also know if he needs a middle-of-the-night potty trip. Whatever you do, do not lend comfort by taking the puppy into bed with you. To a dog, on the bed means equal, which is not a good idea this early on as you are trying to establish yourself as the puppy's leader.

Make a practice of placing your puppy in his crate for naps, at nighttime and whenever you are unable to watch him closely. Not to worry…he will let you know when he wakes up and needs a potty trip. If he falls asleep under the table or on the living-room carpet, guess what he'll do first when he wakes up? Make a puddle, and then toddle over to say "Hi!"

Become a Pembroke vigilante. Puppies always "go" when they wake up (quickly now!), within a few minutes after eating, after play periods and after brief periods of confinement. Also be aware of his water intake. Here's a house-training hint: remove the puppy's water after 7 PM to aid in nighttime bladder control. If he gets thirsty, offer him an ice cube. Then just watch him race for the refrigerator when he hears the rattle of the ice-cube tray.

Most pups under 12 weeks of age will need to eliminate at least every hour or so, or up to 10 times a day (set your oven timer to remind you). Routines, consistency and an eagle eye are your keys to house-training success. Always take the puppy outside on his leash to the same area, telling him "Outside" as you go out. Pick a "potty" word ("Hurry up," "Go

Potty" and "Get Busy" are some that are commonly used), and use it when he does his business, lavishing him with "Good puppy" praise and repeating your keyword. Always use the same exit door for these potty trips and confine puppy to the exit area so he can find the door when he needs it. When he goes to the door, don't delay. Put his leash on and get him outside.

Of course, puppy will have accidents. All puppies do. If you catch him in the act, clap your hands loudly, say "Aaah! Aaah!" and scoop him up to go outside. Your voice should startle him and make him stop (don't worry if he still drips a little as you carry him). Be sure to praise when he finishes his duty outside.

If you discover the piddle spot after the fact—more than three or four seconds later—you're too late. Pups only understand *in the moment,* and will not understand a correction given more than five

(yes, only five) seconds after the deed. Correcting any later will only cause fear and confusion. Just forget it and vow to be more vigilant. Never,

and I mean *never*, rub your puppy's nose in his mistake or strike your puppy or adult dog with your hand, a newspaper or another object to correct him. He will not understand your "message" and will only become fearful of the person who is hitting him.

Despite its many benefits, crate use can be abused. Puppies under 12 weeks of age should never be confined for more than 2 hours at a time,

If you have a fenced yard, eventually you will be able to let your Corgi out on his own to do his business in the proper area.

unless, of course, they are sleeping. A general rule of thumb is three hours maximum for a three-month-old pup, four to five hours for the four- to five-month-old pup and no more than six hours for dogs over six

Know how to use the crate properly so that it will be an effective training and safety tool, never a place of punishment or overly long periods of confinement.

months of age. If you're unable to be home to release the dog, arrange for a relative, neighbor or dog-sitter to let him out to exercise and potty.

One final, but most important, rule of crate use: never, *ever* use the crate for punishment. Successful crate use depends on your puppy's positive association with his "house." If the crate represents punishment or "bad dog stuff," he will resist using it as his safe place. Sure, you can crate your pup to keep him from getting underfoot as you clean up after he has sorted through the trash. Just don't do it in an angry fashion or tell him "Bad dog, crate!" Wait a few minutes, then happily place him in the crate with a treat while you clean up the mess.

Once your puppy becomes more reliable in his potty behavior and behavior in general, you may want to progress to letting him stay alone in one room, closed off with baby gates or another dog-proof barrier. Completely puppy-proof the room by removing anything that your pup could chew or damage and hurt himself in the process. Even in a stripped environment, though, some pups will chew through drywall or find other ways to amuse themselves if bored. An exercise pen 4 feet by 4 feet square (available through pet suppliers), sturdy enough that the pup can't knock it down and high enough that he can't climb out, will provide safe containment for short periods. Place his crate in the room or pen (if the pen is large enough), as he will probably go into the crate on his own to nap. Safe chew toys should help keep him happy and safely occupied while you're gone.

Whichever method you choose, remember that successful house-training revolves around consistency and repetition, just like any other type of training. Maintain a strict schedule and use your keywords consistently. Well-trained owners have well-trained pups...and clean, nice-smelling houses!

HOUSE-TRAINING AND OTHER BASICS

Overview

- Socialization ensures that your pup will grow up to be well adjusted and will behave politely in all sorts of situations.
- A puppy class is a worthwhile experience for both socialization and getting started with basic commands.
- House-training, which means to teach the puppy proper toileting habits, will begin on day one.
- Crate-training is the most effective way to house-train; proper use of the dog crate also has many more benefits related to your pup's training and safety.
- Be consistent in house-training with your timing and praise. Never use the crate for punishment.

CHAPTER 8

Teaching Basic Commands

You will find it to your advantage to have a mannerly dog. With a Corgi, basic training should begin right away. Pembrokes are intelligent dogs and will take over the "alpha" role if you do not establish yourself as boss from the outset. There are some important basic commands that your dog must understand, not just to make him a better citizen, but for his safety as well. One of the family members should attend

"Stay" is one of the basic commands that your Pembroke must learn. In all commands, start out with your dog on leash; only attempt off-leash training in an enclosed area and only once your dog is reliable with performing the command on leash.

puppy kindergarten classes with the pup. You will cover the basics, like sit, heel, down, stay and come (or recall). There are definite advantages to each. Sit and heel are great helps when walking your dog. Who needs a puppy walking between your legs, lunging forward or lagging behind, acting like a nut? Have your dog walking like a gentleman on your left side and sitting as you wait to cross the street. The come, or recall, is the most important of commands for your dog's safety. In the unfortunate event that he should get away from you, you will need him to respond reliably to your call to return to you.

To show your Corgi what is expected of him when you say "Sit," a little gentle pressure on the rump will guide him into the correct position.

Here is a short rundown of the basic and other helpful commands. If you attend puppy classes or obedience training classes, you will have professional help in learning these commands. However, you and your dog can learn these very basic exercises on your own.

Treats are very effective rewards. Most dogs jump for joy at the sight of a tasty tidbit.

SIT

This is the first exercise you should teach. Stand in front of your pup, move the treat directly over his nose and slowly move it backwards over his head. As he folds backwards to reach the goodie, his rear end will move downward to the floor. If the puppy raises up or stands to reach the treat, just lower it a bit. The moment his behind is down, tell him to "Sit." That's one word, "Sit." Give him the treat and praise: "Good sit!"

Sit is recommended as the first command to teach because it is easy and your Pembroke will learn it quickly.

As he becomes more proficient, make him hold the sit position longer before you give the treat (this is the beginning of the stay command). Begin using a release word like "Okay" to release him from the sit position. Practice using the command for things like sitting for his food bowl or a toy, and do random sits throughout the day. Make a game of it, always for a food or praise "prize."

STAY

Teach your dog to stay in a seated position until you call him. Have your dog sit and, as you say "Stay," place your hand in front of his nose and take a step or two, no more at the beginning, away. Wait just a few seconds and then call your dog. If he gets up before the end of the command, have him sit again and repeat the stay command. When he stays until called (remembering to start with a very short distance and period of time), praise him and give him a treat. As he learns this command, increase the distance that you move away from the dog as well as the length of time that he stays.

HEEL

The formal heel command comes a bit later in the learning curve. A young

The basic commands build a foundation for more advanced obedience exercises. In off-leash heeling, the dog begins and ends at the owner's left side in the sit position.

Pembroke should be taught simply to walk politely on a leash, at or near your side. Start leash training soon after your pup comes home. Simply attach his leash to his buckle collar and let him drag it around for a little while every day. Play a puppy game with the leash on. Make wearing his leash a happy moment in his day. If he chews the leash, distract him with a play activity. You also can spray the leash with a bitter-tasting chew-deterrent product to make it taste unpleasant and therefore undesirable to chew.

After a few days, gather up the leash in a distraction-free zone of the house or yard and take just a few steps together. With your puppy on your left side, hold a treat lure at his eye level to encourage the puppy to walk next to you. Pat your knee and use a happy voice. Use the phrase "Let's go!" as you move forward, holding the treat low to keep him near. Take a few steps, give the treat and praise. Move forward just a few steps each time.

Keep these sessions short and happy (30 seconds is a lot in puppy time). Never scold him or nag him into walking faster or slower, just encourage him with happy talk. Walk straight ahead at first, adding wide turns once he gets the hang of it. Progress to 90-degree turns, using a gentle leash tug on the turns, a happy verbal "Let's go!" and, of course, a treat. Walk in short 10- to 20-second bursts with a happy break (use your release word) and brief play (nothing wild or crazy, hugs will do nicely) in between. Keep total training time short and always quit with success, even if just a few short steps. Formal heeling will come much later with advanced instruction in a basic obedience class.

DOWN

Down can be a tough command to master. Because the down position is a submissive one, some dogs and certain take-charge breeds may find it especially difficult. That's why it's most important to teach this command to dogs when they are very young. The older they get, the more difficult it will be.

From the sit position, move the food lure from his nose to the ground and slightly backwards between his front paws. Wiggle the treat as necessary to attract the pup's attention. As soon as his front legs and rear end hit the floor, give the treat and tell him "Down, good boy, down" to connect the word to the

behavior. "Down" may prove difficult, so be patient and generous with the praise when he cooperates. Once he goes into the down position with ease, incorporate the stay as you did with sit. By six months of age, your puppy should be able to do a ten-minute solid sit/stay, ditto for a down/stay.

COME (RECALL)

This command has life-saving potential. If your Pembroke were to run into the street, go

Your index finger pointing toward the ground is sometimes used as a hand signal along with the verbal command "Down." Always be gentle and reassuring when teaching this exercise.

after a squirrel, chase a child on a bike, break his leash or otherwise get away from you, you need to be able to call him back. This command is the most important for your Pembroke's safety.

Always practice the come command on leash and in a safely confined area. You can't afford to risk failure or the pup will learn that he does not have to come when called. Once you have the pup's attention, call him from a short distance: "Puppy, come!" (use your happy voice) and give a treat when he comes to you. If he hesitates, tug him to you gently with his leash. Grasp and hold his collar with one hand as you dispense the treat. The collar grasp is important. You will eventually phase out the treat and switch to hands-on praise only. This maneuver also connects holding his collar with coming and treating, which will assist you in countless future behaviors.

Do 10 or 12 repetitions 2 or 3 times a day. Once your pup has mastered the come on his leash, you can progress to using a long line, such as a lightweight rope that is 10 or 12 feet long. Continue to practice daily to imprint this most important behavior onto his tiny brain. You can progress to practicing off-leash in your fenced yard only when he is reliably responding to the command on a long line.

Experienced owners know, however, that you can never completely trust a dog to come when called if the dog is bent on a self-appointed mission. Off-leash is often synonymous with out of control. Thus, for his safety, always keep your Pembroke Welsh Corgi on leash when not in a fenced or confined area. If he should get away from you and you need to call him back, do so calmly yet firmly, not in a nervous or overly excited tone that will in turn make the dog nervous.

WAIT

Work on the wait command with a closed interior door. (It would not be wise to try this with a door that opens to the outdoors.) Start to open the door as if to go through or out. When your puppy tries to follow, step in front and body-block him to prevent his passage. Don't use the actual command just yet, but keep blocking until he hesitates and you can open the door a little to pass through. Then say your release word, "Through," "Okay" or whatever release word you have chosen for this exercise, and let him go through the door. Repeat by body-blocking until he understands and waits for you, then start applying the word "Wait" to the behavior.

TAKE IT AND LEAVE IT

Place a treat in the palm of your hand and tell your puppy to "Take it" as he grabs the treat. Repeat three times. On the fourth time, do not say a word as your dog reaches for the treat, just close your fingers around the treat and wait. Do not pull away, but be prepared for the pup to paw, lick, bark

Take it and leave it are commands not just for polite manners but also for your Pembroke's safety. Think of how many things you do not want him to pick up off the ground!

and nibble on your fingers. Patience! When he finally pulls away from your hand and waits for a few seconds, open your hand and tell him to "Take it."

Now for the next step. Show your Pembroke the treat in the palm of your hand and tell him to "Leave it." When he goes for the treat, close your hand and repeat "Leave it." Repeat the process until he pulls away, then wait just a second, open your hand, tell him to "Take it" and allow him to take the treat. Repeat the "Leave it" process until he waits just a few seconds, then give the treat on "Take it." Gradually extend the time you wait after your puppy "Leaves it" and before you tell him to "Take it."

OTHER HELPFUL COMMANDS
There are some commands that are not taught in obedience class that you and your dog will learn on your own. "Off " is an important command, as with a bouncy Corgi, even with his short legs, he can be active and agile enough to reach the candy dish on the coffee table or jump on the new and expensive sofa. "Off, Geoff" and then guide him down on his four feet. Again, dogs are smart, particularly Corgis, and he will quickly learn what "Off" means as long as you are consistent.

It's also helpful to use commands to tell your Pembroke that it's time to go to his crate. For example, "Kennel up" and "Bedtime" are different commands with different meanings. "Kennel up" is used when you are going out to run an errand or out to dinner or the like. "Bedtime" means that he is getting his nighttime treat and going in the crate for the night. Don't confuse the two, as your Pembroke will learn to differentiate between the two crate commands.

Of course, the most basic of commands, which is learned

very quickly, is "No." Say it firmly and with conviction. Your dog will learn that "No" means to keep off, don't do it or don't even think about it!

KEEP PRACTICING

A big part of training is patience, persistence and routine. Teach each command the same way every time. Do not lose your patience with the dog, as he will not understand what you are doing. Reward your dog for performing his commands properly, sometimes with treats but always with praise. With a

Corgi, you will find that your puppy will learn the basic commands very quickly. And do remember, the Corgi can be a willful dog, one who will take charge if you do not. It is essential that you teach him early on that manners are important. Not only will you enjoy your well-trained family member, but your friends, when they come to your house for a dinner party, will also appreciate a well-behaved dog who will not jump on their clothing or land in their laps while they are having cocktails.

TEACHING BASIC COMMANDS

Overview

- Knowledge of the basic commands is essential for your Pembroke's good manners as well as his safety.
- Sit, stay, down, heel and come, the latter with real life-saving potential, are basic commands for any dog.
- For safety and effective training, begin teaching all commands on leash; progress to off-leash training only in enclosed areas and only once the command is learned reliably on leash.
- Other very helpful commands include take it/leave it, wait, no, off and commands to tell your puppy that it's crate time.

Home Care of Your Pembroke

Show your Pembroke how much you and your family love him by being diligent about his healthcare in between veterinary visits.

Ask any dog owner—his dog's life is too doggone short. Our beloved pets will not outlive us, and the pain of losing them is excruciating. But there are many things that we as owners can do to maintain them in the best possible health, maximize their life expectancy and help them live out their years in health and comfort. Adult dogs generally have annual physical exams and more frequent veterinary visits as they age, but in between those trips to the veterinarian, we are our dogs' healthcare providers at home.

The average Pembroke lives about 12 to 14 years, but there are many cases of Corgis living much longer, up to 16 and 17 years. The quality of those years depends on a conscientious home healthcare program. Although genetics and the environment certainly can influence a dog's longevity, the fact remains that you are the backbone of your Pembroke's health-maintenance program. Like the proverbial apple-a-day, your daily focus on canine wellness will help "keep the veterinarian away."

Dental care is one of the most important aspects of your dog's home healthcare routine. Tooth and gum disease can cause very serious problems, but can be prevented with attention to your dog's dental health.

WEIGHT CONTROL

Veterinarians tell us that over 50% of the dogs they see are grossly overweight and that such obesity will take two to three years off a dog's life, given the strain it puts on the animal's heart, lungs and joints. The obvious message here is that lean is healthier; this cannot be ignored.

When your Pembroke pup comes home with you, you are committing to providing him with the healthcare he needs for the rest of his life.

Keep a record of your Pembroke's weight from each vet visit. A few extra pounds? Adjust his food portions (watch those treats!), perhaps switch to a "light," "senior" or lower calorie dog-food formula and increase his exercise. You should be able to see a "waist" when looking at your dog from above, and his belly should have a moderate tuck-up. A hands-on evaluation will also reveal if your Corgi has a too-thick layer of fat.

ORAL HYGIENE

Now that your dog is slim and trim, let's examine his teeth. The American Veterinary Dental Society states that 80% of dogs show signs of oral disease as early as age 3. Further studies prove that good oral hygiene can add three to five years to a dog's life. Need I say more? (Quick, look at your dog's teeth!) Dental care is an essential home-care regimen.

Danger signs include yellow and brown build-up of tartar along the gumline, red inflamed gums and persistent bad breath. If neglected, these conditions will allow bacteria to accumulate in your dog's mouth and enter your dog's bloodstream through those damaged gums, increasing the risk for disease in vital organs such as the heart, liver and kidneys. It's also known that periodontal disease is a major contributor to kidney disease, which is a common cause of death in older dogs and highly preventable.

Your vet should examine your Pembroke's teeth and gums during his annual check-ups to make sure they are clean and healthy. He may recommend a professional veterinary cleaning if there is excessive plaque build-up. During the other 364 days of the year, you are your dog's dentist. Brush his teeth daily, or at least twice a week. Use a doggie toothbrush (designed for the contour of a canine's mouth) and use canine tooth-paste flavored with chicken, beef or liver (minty people paste is harmful to dogs). If your dog resists a toothbrush, try a nappy washcloth or gauze pad wrapped around your finger. Start the brushing process with gentle gum massages when your Pembroke is very young so he will learn to tolerate and even enjoy getting his teeth cleaned.

LUMPS, BUMPS AND BUGS

Your weekly grooming sessions should include body checks for lumps (cysts, warts and fatty tumors), hot spots and other skin or coat problems. While harmless skin lumps are common in older dogs, many can be malignant, and your vet should examine any abnormality. Black mole-like patches or growths on any body part require immediate veterinary inspection.

Remember, petting and hugging also can turn up little abnormalities.

Fleas have been around for centuries, and it's likely that you will wage a flea battle sometime during your Pembroke's lifetime. Fortunately, there are quite a few low-toxic, effective flea preventives to aid you and your dog in your war against fleas. Ask your vet about the safest type of preventive for your Corgi.

Three tick-borne diseases, Lyme disease (canine borreliosis), ehrlichiosis and Rocky Mountain spotted fever, are now found in almost every

Start your Pembroke's dental care when he is a puppy with gentle brushing and routine mouth exams so he gets used to this type of handling and will cooperate.

state and can affect humans as well as dogs. Dogs that live in or visit areas where ticks are present, whether seasonally or year-round, must be protected. There are many effective, easy-to-use preventives that protect against both ticks and fleas and can be obtained through your veterinarian.

Clean your Pembroke's ears gently with a cotton ball or pad, never probing into the ear, and make sure that his ears stay healthy-looking and free of debris.

EAR CARE

It's most important to keep your Pembroke's upright ears clean and dry, so have your vet show you the proper way

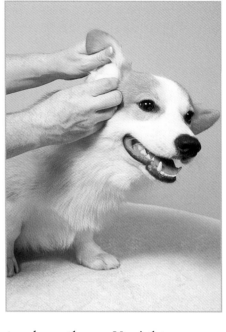

to clean them. Upright ears get better air circulation and are less prone to infection than drop ears, but they also are more prone to having dirt and debris enter them. Check the ears at least weekly. Are they clean and fresh-smelling? Any signs of waxy residue? Your vet may prescribe or recommend an ear-cleaning product that you can use with a cotton ball or pad. Whatever you do, do not probe into the dog's ear canal.

Tear stains or matter collected in the corners of the eyes can be wiped away with a gentle touch and a soft pad or cotton ball. Special cleaning formulas also are available.

EYE CARE

Your Pembroke's vision may deteriorate with age. A bluish haze is common in geriatric dogs and does not impair vision, but you should always check with your vet about any changes in the eyes to determine if they are harmless or indicative of a problem.

THE OTHER END

How about his rear end? Does he chew at his rear or scoot and rub it on the carpet? That's a sign of impacted anal glands. Have your vet express those glands (it's not a job for amateurs). Have annual stool cultures done to check for intestinal parasites. Hook-, whip- and roundworms can cause weight and appetite loss, poor coat quality and all manner of intestinal problems as well as weaken your dog's resistance to other canine diseases.

HOME CARE OF YOUR PEMBROKE

Overview

- You are your dog's healthcare provider in between his visits to the vet.
- Watch your dog's weight! Obesity is a major problem in dogs, compromising the quality of life and leading to other health problems.
- Your dog needs regular dental care just like you do, as neglecting his teeth can lead to gum disease that can progress to serious internal problems.
- Make it part of your routine to check your Pembroke's skin and coat, clean his ears and eyes and check for anal-sac impactions.
- Keep up with your Pembroke's parasite checks and don't forget to give his preventives on schedule.

Feeding the Pembroke Welsh Corgi

Nutrition for your puppy is actually very easy. Dog-food companies hire many scientists and spend millions of dollars on research to determine what will be the most healthy diet for your dog at all stages of life. Your breeder should have been feeding a premium puppy food and you should continue on with the same brand. As the dog matures, you will change over to the adult formula, likely of the same dog-food brand. Do not add vitamins or

The breeder will start the pups off on solid food as part of the weaning process.

anything else unless your veterinarian suggests that you do so. Do not think that by cooking up a special diet you will turn out a product that will be more nutritional than what the dog-food companies are providing.

A proper diet is as important for healthy dogs as it is for healthy people. Only the premium (and usually higher-end) dog foods provide the proper balance of the vitamins, minerals and supplements that are necessary to support healthy bone, muscle, skin and coat. The major dog-food manufac-turers have done extensive research on canine nutrition and developed their formulas with strict controls, using only quality ingredients obtained from reliable sources. The labels on the food packaging detail the products in the food (beef, chicken, corn, etc.), and list ingredients in descending order of weight or amount in the food. You do not want fillers like corn or by-products to be at the top of the list!

Manufactured foods are the most convenient way to provide your Pembroke with complete nutrition at every stage of life.

No dog can resist sticking his nose into the treat jar. Use treats wisely—don't overdo it or allow your Pembroke to help himself!

Rather, look for quality protein sources like beef, chicken and lamb.

Don't be intimidated by all of those dog-food bags on the store shelves. Read the labels on the bags (how else can you learn what's in those foods?) and call the manufacturers' information numbers with any questions you may have. A solid education in the basics of canine nutrition will provide the tools you need to offer your dog a diet that is best for his long-term health.

In the world of quality dog foods, there are enough choices to confuse even experienced dog folks. Today there are specific formulas designed for every breed size, age and activity level. Just like the diet of a human infant differs from that of a human adult, puppies require a diet different than that of an adult canine. Puppy growth formulas contain protein and fat levels that are appropriate for different-sized dogs. A small- to medium-sized dog like your Pembroke requires appropriate amounts of protein and fat to promote healthy joint development. A good puppy food works with the puppy's natural growth rate and does not encourage him to grow too quickly, which can lead to skeletal disorders. As we've mentioned, do not add your own vitamin supplements or table scraps to a nutritionally complete food. You will only upset the balance of the food, which could negatively affect the growth pattern or maintenance of your pup or adult.

Water is an essential component of a healthy diet, so do have a supply of fresh, clean drinking water available to your Pembroke at all times. You may want an additional water bowl to put outdoors when your Pembroke is spending time in the yard. When exercising outdoors, he will surely become thirsty!

WHEN AND HOW MUCH?

Your young puppy will probably be fed three times a day and perhaps as many as four times a day. Dry food switch without causing stomach distress, take away a little of the old food and replace it with the new. Each day, take away a little more

Your individual dog and his activity level will play a part in determining the daily food portions that will keep him in good condition.

should make up the bulk of his portion and you may want to add a tablespoon or two of a quality canned food at each feeding. If you decide to switch to a food other than what the puppy was fed by the breeder, be sure to choose a good-quality premium food. If you skimp on his food quality, you will pay for it later in vet bills. To make a old and add a little more new, and keep increasing the ratio of new food to old food until his portion consists entirely of the new food.

Use the suggested portion amounts on the dog-food packages as a guide to how much to feed your puppy. At around six months of age or so, you will change to a twice-daily feeding schedule. This is the schedule he will stay on as an adult, as it is shown to be healthier for the dog's digestion than one large meal each day. By the time he reaches one year of age, you will be changing over to an adult-maintenance food. Again, use the suggested amounts as a guide for your dog's daily portions. Be aware that usually the recommendations refer to one day's worth

Watch your puppy for any signs of food-guarding behavior. He shouldn't mind your being near his food or even putting your hand in his bowl.

of food, so be sure to divide the daily portion in half: half in the morning and half in the evening. You might want to add water to dry food to moisten it and possibly a bit of a canned dog food for flavor. However, at all life stages, dry kibble is recom-

mended as the main part of the meal, as the crunchy pieces help with plaque and tartar control.

Free-feeding, that is, leaving a bowl of food available all day, is not recommended. Free-feeding fosters picky eating habits...a bite here, a nibble there. Free-feeders are also more likely to become possessive of their food bowls, a problem behavior that signals the beginning of aggression.

Scheduled meals give you one more opportunity to remind your Pembroke that all good things in life come from you, his chef and owner! With scheduled meals, it's also easier to predict elimination, which is the better road to house-training success. Regular meals help you know just how much your puppy eats and when, which is valuable information for weight control or if your dog's appetite changes, which could signal illness.

Allow your dog about 20 minutes to eat his food. Some will eat the whole bowl of food with gusto, while others may take their time and leisurely nibble at the food. If your Pembroke eats his dry food too quickly, a splash of water or a little canned food may help slow him down; gulping his food is not good for his digestion. Remove any food that remains after 20 minutes and do not add it to the next meal. If at any time in your Pembroke's life you feel that he is becoming too picky, discuss that problem with your vet.

LEAN IS IN

Like people, puppies and adult dogs have different appetites; some will lick their food bowls clean and beg for more, while others pick at their food and leave some of it untouched. It's easy to overfeed a "chow-hound." Who can resist those soulful Pembroke eyes? Be strong and stay the right course. Chubby puppies may be cute and cuddly, but the extra weight will stress their growing joints and is thought to be a factor in the development of hip and elbow problems. Overweight pups also tend to grow into overweight adults who tire easily and will be more susceptible to other health problems. If the portion guidelines on the food bag are leaving your pup looking under- or overweight, take advice from your breeder and vet about how to adjust meal portions as your puppy grows.

Always remember that lean is healthy and fat is not. Research has proven that obesity is a major canine killer. Quite simply, a lean dog lives longer than one who is overweight, and that doesn't even reflect the better quality of life for the lean dog that can run, jump and play without the burden of an extra 10 or 20 pounds.

If your adult dog is

overweight, you can switch to a "light" food that has fewer calories and more fiber. "Senior" foods for older dogs are formulated to meet the needs of less active older dogs. "Performance" diets contain more fat and protein for dogs that compete in sporting disciplines or lead very active lives.

TREAT TIPS

All dogs love treats, but use them wisely. Too many treats can be like an additional meal, which will put excess weight on your Pembroke in no time. Crunchy dog biscuits or even small pieces of cooked chicken, cheese or carrots are healthy treats. Other things are not suitable, such as table scraps of any kind, which will likely cause stomach upset and will definitely encourage begging. In fact, certain "people foods," among them chocolate, nuts, raisins, grapes and onions, are actually toxic to dogs. Natural bones are not suitable treats, either; they splinter easily and are quite dangerous, causing choking and intestinal problems if swallowed.

RAW FOODS

To complicate the dog-food dilemma, there are also raw foods available for those who prefer to feed their dogs a completely natural diet rather than traditional manufactured dog food. The debate on raw and/or all-natural vs. manufactured dog food is a

Treats are used in the show ring to keep the dog attentive and alert.

fierce one, with some raw-food proponents claiming that raw diets have cured their dogs' allergies and other chronic ailments. If you are interested in this alternative feeding method, you will have to do some research and read the writings of canine nutrition experts on this topic. You also can check with your vet and/or breeder if either of them has experience with feeding raw-food diets.

YOU ARE WHAT YOU EAT!
The bottom line is this: what and how much you feed your dog are major factors in your Pembroke's overall health and longevity. It's worth your investment in extra time and dollars to provide the best diet for your dog.

FEEDING THE PEMBROKE WELSH CORGI

Overview

- Choose a complete and balanced food for your Pembroke, appropriate to his stage of life and physical condition.
- How to choose? Read the labels, take advice from your breeder and ask your vet; you might even start your pup on the same food he was fed by the breeder.
- The puppy will need more frequent daily feedings than the adult. Regardless, scheduled mealtimes are the best way to feed rather than free-feeding.
- The amounts you feed should keep your Pembroke in fit condition. Use treats wisely, and avoid giving your dog "people food."
- If interested in trying an alternative feeding method, be sure to do your research first so that you know how to safely provide proper nutrition.

Grooming the Pembroke Welsh Corgi

A big plus with the Corgi is that there is only a minimal amount of grooming required, unlike some other breeds that are long-coated or heavily sculpted. Do understand, though, before purchasing your Pembroke, that he will need some grooming and attention to his hygiene. You should start grooming your puppy shortly after bringing him home as he will then

The Pembroke's compact size, sparkling personality and minimal grooming needs often appeal to owners so much that they can't stop with just one!

become used to the routine and will even grow to like the attention. It will be helpful if you have a grooming table with a non-slip surface. The table should have an overhead arm to which you can attach the dog's leash to keep him secure on the table. This is helpful not only for tending to the coat but for trimming toenails and performing other routine tasks. You can also use a countertop or other raised surface where you can place an eye hook above it for attaching the leash. Your dog will be standing for some of his grooming, but other times he will not be leashed to the table and will be lying on his side. Regardless, if using a grooming table or other raised surface, never leave your dog unattended. He could injure himself if he falls or tries to jump off, especially if he is left hanging in mid-air with the leash around his neck.

The grooming tools required for the Pembroke are quite basic. You will need a bristle brush, a steel comb,

During times of heavy shedding, a shedding blade is a very helpful tool in removing dead undercoat. Dead hair must be removed to keep the dog's coat and skin healthy.

All grooming tasks should be started when the Pembroke is a puppy so that he will get used to the routine and will not resist.

toenail clippers and a good pair of scissors. A slicker brush tends to pull out too much coat. To start brushing, you will begin at the neck of the dog and work back to the rear, being sure to brush (or comb) through to the skin and always brush or comb with the lie of the coat. If there should be any small mats, separate them with your fingers and then comb them out. Not brushing through to the skin will give the undercoat a chance to mat, but with a good weekly brushing and comb-through,

you should not have any problems. Corgis will shed twice a year, usually most heavily in the spring and then again in the fall, during which times the coat will drop fairly rapidly. If you have any problems during this period, a shedding blade or undercoat rake will help to pull out the loose coat. It is important to remove the dead hair from the coat.

Laying the dog on his side will help you get all of the hard-to-reach and more sensitive areas, like the

Some owners use a light mist of water or conditioning spray over the coat before brushing to minimize hair breakage.

"armpits" and under the chest. Do one side, and then turn the dog over to do the other side. Don't forget to brush the "pants" on the legs. Brush a small section at a time, brushing downward toward the feet.

After a thorough brush-through, repeat with your comb. You can even gently comb the face and head areas. You may wish to finish up by using your blunt-ended scissors to neaten up around the feet, being careful not to nip the skin in between the toes. You may also want to trim your Pembroke's whiskers, but this is a matter of personal preference. Remember, this is a natural breed and that's how you want him to look even after a full grooming. This is one of the traits that make the Pembroke very appealing…it doesn't take much to keep him looking in top condition!

After your Pembroke's weekly brushing would be a

Brushing the coat should become a pleasant part of your regular routine with your Corgi pal.

good time to check and clean his ears and eyes, as we've mentioned that this is an important part of your dog's home care. You also should check your dog's nails and clip them as needed, starting in puppyhood so that your dog is used to the process. Purchase a quality toenail trimmer for pets. You may want to purchase a styptic stick in case you trim the nail too short and bleeding starts. If your dog's toenails are light in color, you will easily see the blood vessel (the "quick") inside the nail. However, the quick is a bit more difficult to see in dark-toed dogs and you may nick the blood vessel until you are more familiar with trimming the nails. Clip just a little at a time. You should also check the footpads to make sure they are not cracked and nothing has become embedded in them.

BATHING YOUR CORGI

How often should you bathe your Pembroke? Frequent bathing is seldom necessary, and, in fact, will remove the essential oils that keep your dog's skin supple and his coat soft and gleaming. Bathe him with a good conditioning shampoo about twice a year, or more often if he plays in mud holes or rolls around in something smelly (a favorite outdoor pastime.)

Bathing rituals can be a challenge if your dog dislikes water or getting lathered up. To minimize the stress and struggle of bath time, start when your pup is small. Lure your puppy into the tub with food rewards, perhaps something special like squirt cheese or peanut butter. Line the tub or shower with a towel or rubber mat for safe footing. Start with a dry tub, and after the pup is comfortable there, gradually add shallow water and then begin to bathe him. He may never learn to love it, but all you need is his cooperation.

Use only a shampoo made

A slicker brush can be helpful during shedding times, but is not recommended for routine brushing as it can remove too much coat.

for dogs, working it into a good lather and then rinsing thoroughly. Always be sure to rinse the coat completely to avoid any itching from residual shampoo. A good chamois is the ideal tool for drying, as it absorbs water like a sponge. Keep your dog away from drafts for a good while after bathing and drying to prevent chilling. Once the initial moisture is absorbed from the coat, you can use a blow dryer to finish drying, either your own on the lowest heat setting or a dryer made for use on dogs. Comb through the coat as you dry, combing and directing the air with the lie of the hair.

Spritz-on or powder dry shampoos are handy in case you need a quick clean-up to remove dirt and body odor. Pre-moistened bath wipes also are available for a quick freshening of the coat.

GROOMING THE PEMBROKE WELSH CORGI

Overview

- The Pembroke has minimal grooming needs. His coat care needs are basic: regular brushing and combing at least once a week and bathing as needed.
- Start all grooming tasks when your Pembroke is a puppy so that he is used to the routine and cooperates with you.
- During your Pembroke's twice-yearly times of shedding, he will need more attention to his coat as all of the dead hair must be removed.
- Other routine maintenance tasks include clipping your dog's nails, cleaning his ears and cleaning around his eyes.
- Bathing too often is drying to the skin and coat, so this only should be done about twice a year unless the need for additional baths arises.

Keeping the Pembroke Active

Y ou will not have a problem keeping your Pembroke active, as they are very active dogs! They love to run and play (particularly with their owners), and they love to entertain and to keep themselves entertained.

There are many activities to keep you and your Corgi very busy, active and challenged. One of the most obvious pursuits for a Pembroke is competitive herding. Herding tests and trials are not offered all over the country, but you can check with the various clubs to see if there are any held in your region. Clubs that

The athletic Corgi can run, jump, weave and climb with the best of them in agility trials. The jump heights are adjusted for different-sized dogs so that every breed can participate with success.

hold herding events for the various herding breeds are the AKC, the American Herding Breeds Association and the Australian Shepherd Club of America. In addition, some Pembroke Welsh Corgi clubs offer herding events. Your individual Corgi may or may not be interested, but this may be just his cup of tea.

The weave poles are another agility exercise; it's quite a sight to see a dog navigate this obstacle with speed and dexterity.

After you and your Corgi have completed puppy kindergarten class, you may want to work toward an AKC Canine Good Citizen® award. This is a program that, when successfully completed, shows that your dog will mind his manners at home, in public places and with other dogs. This class is available to all dogs, pure-bred and mixed breeds alike, of any age.

The ten steps are accepting a friendly stranger, sitting politely for petting, accepting light grooming and examination from a stranger, walking on a loose lead, coming when called, responding calmly to another dog,

Consider competing with your Corgi at conformation shows. Dog shows are the most elegant and prestigious of all canine competitions.

responding to distractions, down on command and remaining calm when the owner is out of sight for three minutes. Upon successful completion, your Pembroke will receive an AKC Canine Good Citizen® certificate and the CGC suffix to add to his name. From here, you may even want to progress to training for competitive obedience.

The quick and athletic little Corgi can fare well in agility competition, basically an "obstacle course" for dogs. There are a number of titles to be earned in agility, depending upon the obstacles that the dog

Here's Best-in-Show-winning Ch. Coventry Queue, the top Corgi bitch in history, with 71 Best-in-Show victories.

is able to conquer. The AKC defines agility as: "The enjoyment of bringing together communication, training, timing, accuracy and just plain fun in the ultimate game for you and your dog." It's lots of enjoyment and exercise for both dog and owner, and there is great joy in watching the smart-looking Pembroke race through his paces! You will find it a pleasure to work agility with your Corgi!

For a very rewarding activity that is not competitive, you and your Pembroke Welsh Corgi might train for pet therapy work. Corgis can excel as therapy dogs, visiting places like nursing homes, hospitals or assisted living centers for an hour or two, usually once a week, so that the dogs can visit and bring companionship and comfort to the patients and residents there. Different organizations offer testing and certification for therapy dogs, which will be necessary.

In addition to the organized

activities that we've discussed, there is plenty that you can do with your Pembroke at home to keep him busy and happy. Corgis of all ages like to play interactive games with their toys, like tug, fetch or catch. A puppy will naturally chase after a ball that is thrown, and you can encourage your pup to return the toy to you. Of course we know that Pembrokes are herders, not retrievers, but any dog can be taught to bring an object to his owner. Corgis have even been known to play with a ball by themselves, pushing it along the floor or from the top of the stairs and then running to retrieve it. Never give him a toy or ball that is small enough for him to swallow, as he will swallow it, requiring an emergency trip to the vet.

Of course, the easiest way to keep your dog active and fit is to take him for good walks every morning and evening. This will be good for you, too! All of the things that you do with your Pembroke to keep him active will build your bond with each other. Isn't companionship and fun part of the reason why you got a dog in the first place?

KEEPING THE PEMBROKE ACTIVE

Overview

- The Pembroke has the potential for success in many areas of competition, among them herding events, obedience and agility.
- AKC Canine Good Citizen® certification is a program that rewards all-around good manners and reliable behavior.
- Your Pembroke's friendly nature and compact size make him a natural for pet therapy work.
- The Pembroke loves to stay active by playing games and having fun with his owners. Additionally, regular walks benefit the two of you, giving you exercise and important bonding time.

Your Pembroke and His Vet

I t's important to connect with a good veterinarian before you bring your puppy home. Your breeder, if from your area, should be able to recommend someone; otherwise, it will be your job to find a clinic that you like. The vet will be your dog's primary healthcare provider, so check with your breeder, your dog-owning friends or your local kennel club for references. A good vet will plan your puppy's long-term health-care and help you become dog-smart about canine healthcare issues.

A healthy, well-cared-for Pembroke is blessed with the potential to live 15 years or even longer, often retaining his keenness and zest for life well into his senior years.

Take your puppy to your veterinarian within three or four days after you bring him home. His tail should already be docked and his dewclaws removed by the breeder, so you might ask your vet to check both. Show the vet any health records of shots and wormings from your breeder. The vet will conduct a thorough physical exam to make sure your Pembroke pup is in good health and will work out a schedule for vaccinations, microchipping and regular visits. A good vet will be gentle and affectionate with a new pup. Keep all health records, and record all health information, especially after every vet visit, so you won't forget it. Also find out if your vet offers emergency services and ask about the clinic's emergency hours. You should also find the phone number of a nearby 24-hour emergency clinic to keep handy with your regular veterinarian's information.

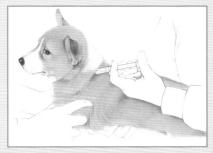

Your vet will pick up with the pup's vaccinations where the breeder left off and will manage your Pembroke's booster-shot schedule throughout the dog's life.

The Pembroke revels in time spent outdoors, so let him enjoy it. Just be diligent in checking his skin and coat often for any signs of problems such as allergies, rashes, insect bites, parasites and the like.

VACCINES

Vaccine protocol for puppies varies with many veterinarians, but most recommend a series of three "combination" shots given at three- to four-week intervals. Your puppy should have had his first shot before he left his breeder. "Combination" shots vary, and a single injection may contain six, seven or even eight vaccines in one shot. Many breeders and veterinarians feel the potency of five or more vaccines in a single shot can negatively compromise a puppy's immature immune system, so they recommend fewer vaccines in one shot or even separating vaccines into individual injections.

The vaccines recommended by the American Veterinary Medical Association (AVMA) are those which protect against diseases most dangerous to your puppy and adult dog. Called core vaccines, these include distemper, canine parvovirus, canine adenovirus (CAV-2) and canine hepatitis (CAV-1). These are generally given together in a combination shot. Rabies immunization is required by law in all 50 states and is given separately.

Vaccines no longer routinely recommended by the AVMA, except when the risk is present, are canine parainfluenza, leptospirosis, canine coron-avirus, bordetella (kennel cough) and Lyme disease (borreliosis). Your vet will alert you if you need to immunize for any of these.

Research suggests that annual vaccinations may actually be over-vaccinating and may be responsible for many of today's canine health problems. Mindful of that, the revised AVMA brochure on vaccinations suggests that vets and owners consider a dog's individual needs before they give booster vaccinations. Many dog owners now do titer tests to check their dogs' antibody levels rather than automatically revaccinating for parvo or distemper.

CHECK-UPS

Regardless of vaccine frequency, every Pembroke should visit his veterinarian at least once a year. At the very least, he needs an annual heartworm test before he can receive another year of heartworm preventive medication. Most importantly, the annual visit keeps your vet apprised of your pet's health progress, and the hands-on exam often turns up small abnormalities that the lay person can't see or feel.

As your Pembroke reaches his senior years, around eight years old, or as the vet recommends it, he should start to visit the vet twice annually. Older dogs are more prone to health problems, like heart disease, kidney disease and cancer, and more frequent visits allow the vet more chances to catch problems early on and thus implement an effective treatment routine.

HEARTWORM

This is a parasite that will ultimately kill your dog. Heartworms grow quite long and wrap themselves around the dog's heart. Now found in all 50 states, heartworm is acquired through a mosquito bite. Even indoor dogs should take heartworm preventive, which can be given daily or monthly in pill form. Heartworm preventive is a prescription medication available only through your veterinarian; many heartworm preventives also protect your dog from other types of internal parasites. Ivermectin, a common preventive, has proven dangerous in some Collies, and

A peaceful nap after a long day of Corgi activity!

some feel that it is risky for any herding dog, so do discuss this with your vet.

SPAY/NEUTER
Spay/neuter is one of the best health-insurance policies you can give your Pembroke. Statistics prove that females spayed before their first heat cycle (estrus) have a 90% lower risk of several common female cancers and other serious problems. Males neutered before their male hormones kick in, usually before six months of age, enjoy greatly reduced risk to zero risk of testicular and prostate cancer and other related tumors and infections. Additionally, neutered males will be less apt to roam, become aggressive or display overt male behaviors.

Having your Pembroke sexually altered will not automatically make him or her fat and lazy. Statistically, having your pet spayed or neutered will make a positive contribution to the pet overpopulation problem and, very importantly, to your dog's long-term health.

YOUR PEMBROKE AND HIS VET

Overview

- Find a good vet before your puppy comes home and plan a visit in your first few days together. Also find the nearest emergency vet clinic and have contact information handy.
- Your vet will continue your puppy's vaccination program and will advise you of when booster shots are due throughout your dog's life.
- Your adult dog's yearly check-ups, and more frequent check-ups as he ages, are important in helping the vet notice any problems as early as possible.
- Your vet will perform fecal tests for internal parasites as well as check his coat for external parasites and will prescribe safe preventives to protect from both.